MAMA IN CONGRESS
Rashida Tlaib's Journey to Washington

RASHIDA AND ADAM TLAIB
with MIRANDA PAUL · Illustrated by OLIVIA ASERR

CLARION BOOKS
An Imprint of HarperCollinsPublishers

Sometimes my little brother, Yousif, and I go to work with our mom.

She's a U.S. congressperson. That means she works in the Capitol Building in Washington, D.C.

When you walk through the Capitol doors, you enter a giant hall that looks like a museum. It feels like anything is possible.

My mom and I want everyone to feel this way, too.

Mama's story of opening doors started long before she was elected to Congress, though.

It began before she was born, when her yama and yaba made their way from Palestine's West Bank to the United States of America. They settled into a new home in southwest Detroit, Michigan. Not long after, they welcomed their first child—a little girl named Rashida.

Soon the house was filled with more kids—my aunts and uncles. Rashida helped her yama cook and care for the younger ones. She choreographed dances and played basketball with them. Eventually there would be fourteen children in all.

That's enough players for two whole teams!

Every now and then, when no one
needed anything, Rashida would take
a few moments to be all by herself.
Sometimes she shut the bedroom
door tight and danced like a pop star.

Other times she laced up her shoes and
ran down the street toward a truck
called the Bookmobile. The books inside
were like wide-open doors to new
worlds, real and imaginary.

DETROIT PUBLIC LIBRARY
BOOKMOBILE

Sometimes when cousins came over to visit, they held their noses. Nearby factories polluted the whole neighborhood with a strong odor, like rotten eggs. The smell got into everyone's clothes and hair. Rashida was used to it, but she still felt embarrassed.

When she traveled with her family, Rashida felt different from kids who lived in other neighborhoods. Some families drove shiny new cars that didn't break down. They didn't eat powdered eggs or rely on government assistance to make sure everyone was fed. The kids in those families wore new clothes and didn't have to share a bedroom with six siblings.

Every now and then, when Rashida and her yama went shopping, cashiers made fun of Yama's accent. One ordered her to "learn English," even though she already spoke it well.

Rashida loved her community and who she was. But as she got older, she worried that students like her would have fewer opportunities. So when Mrs. Marshall asked her to join the high school debate team, she signed up right away.

At her first competition, she looked out at the kids from those other neighborhoods and froze. She had a great argument prepared, but her voice wouldn't push out one word. Her debate partner was confused, then furious. They lost. Why hadn't she said anything?

She felt like she shrunk an inch or two that day.

But that night, she got angry at herself, and at the inequality that made her feel less important in the first place. That anger pushed her to work harder and try again.

A year later, she helped her team win the championship!

Rashida became the first in her family to graduate from high school, college, and law school. She learned more about her faith—Islam—and the reasons behind the traditions her family had followed when she was growing up. She learned how important it is to feel gratitude for what you have, even if you have little.

Her favorite passage from the Quran became "With hardship comes ease."

By then, her brothers and sisters were old enough to take care of themselves. Rashida was ready to start opening doors for other people who had grown up poor or been treated unfairly. She began attending protests. She worked for organizations that helped other immigrant families. Eventually she got a job at the office of Steve Tobocman, an elected official from the Michigan House of Representatives.

Oh, I almost forgot my favorite part! In the middle of these years, my mom gave birth to a bright baby boy named Adam. (That's me!)

Some people believed that women couldn't work and raise a family, but my mother disagreed. She knew how to manage a busy schedule. And helping others was her specialty. So she kept working for Steve as they shaped new laws or changed unfair ones.

When Steve's term limit was up and it was time for another person to take over the job, he said my mom should run for the position.

Mama was surprised at the idea. No Muslim had ever been elected to the Michigan House of Representatives. Some people couldn't even pronounce our last name. (It's Ta-leeb, by the way.) Even her own yaba believed that people wouldn't vote for an Arab, because of untrue stereotypes and unfounded fears.

She recited the Salat al-Istikhara prayer, hoping Allah would provide the answer.

She talked with friends and advisors, and she did a lot of thinking.

She thought of people from her neighborhood who got sick from breathing in the pollution—and how powerful leaders and corporations didn't seem too concerned about stopping it.

She remembered how the cashiers had made fun of her yama's accent. How her parents and so many others had struggled to feed their families.

My mom realized how many people she could help if she won.

Soon we were out on the campaign trail. I was only three, but I remember Mom carried me a lot. Her team visited almost every house in our district twice over a few months.

Knock, knock!
Some people opened their doors and told us their stories or problems that they needed help with.

Knock, knock!
Some people invited us in and said they'd be voting for my mom.

Knock, kn–

Some people slammed the door in our faces.

When I close my eyes, I can still feel that *thump*.

Not everyone believed that my mom should have the opportunity to represent them, and some of them sure weren't nice about it.

But when election day finally came, she won! My mom was the first Muslim woman ever elected to the Michigan House of Representatives!

She worked there for many years, helping to pass new laws and get our neighbors things that they needed—like driver's licenses for immigrants.

And as a lawyer, she worked for a group that challenged the polluting factories and helped make the environment cleaner and safer.

Hey, over here! Don't forget me!

I suppose I should tell you that my brother, Yousif, had come along by then, too.

When I was twelve, Mama decided to try running
for an elected position again—this time for
the U.S. House of Representatives. If she won,
she'd represent Wayne County neighborhoods,
the community that raised her, all the way in
Washington, D.C.

This time, Yousif and I were old enough to help knock on doors and listen to what people thought. And our aunts and uncles—Mom's younger brothers and sisters—jumped in to help, too. My uncle Rachid even drove around in his golf cart delivering flyers and asking people to vote for her.

On election night, we got to stay up really late. The race was close. But the next morning we learned . . .

. . . our mom won!

On the day of her inauguration, Mom put on her special Palestinian thobe. She was one of the first two Muslim women to be elected to the House of Representatives. Our country had set a record for the most women and people of color who would serve in Congress. We were so excited and proud!

Being the first and opening doors for others to follow can be hard, too. On Mom's very first day at her new job, someone threatened her.

People sent our family hateful messages. I thought it would be safer to hide the fact that we were Muslim, if anyone asked.

But Mom says it's important to be
our authentic selves.

Even though it's scary, she keeps
working to help the planet and people,
especially those who need it the most.

When you walk through the U.S. Capitol doors, you enter a giant hall that looks like a museum. It feels like anything is possible.

Mama, why are you one of the first Muslim women in Congress?

Because of people like my mom—and all those who came before, who never gave up—a whole world of doors are starting to open.

And young people like us are ready to walk through them and accomplish great things.

GLOSSARY

cabinet: A group of leaders in the executive branch of government who give advice to the president

campaign: A set of organized plans and actions to reach a goal, such as spreading a message or winning an election

campaign trail: The places visited and events organized by a team

congress: A large group of elected officials whose main jobs are to write and vote on new laws, also referred to as a legislature or part of the legislative branch of government

district: A defined area in which the residents share the same elected officials

elected official: A person who earned enough votes to represent their district, state, or group within the government

federal: Having to do with the United States as a central government or nation, not individual states

inauguration: A ceremony that marks the start of a person's term as an elected official

Salat al-Istikhara: A prayer to ask for guidance or help in making a decision

term: A set amount of time

term limit: The maximum amount of time that an elected official may serve in their position

thobe: A traditional Palestinian dress that is handmade and embroidered

veto: To reject or postpone a decision or proposal

* The portrait that Rashida, Adam, and Yousif walk past in the Capitol Building toward the end of the book is of Shirley Chisholm, the first African American woman elected to Congress, who represented New York State in the U.S. House of Representatives for seven terms.

WHAT DOES THE U.S. GOVERNMENT LOOK LIKE?

You might imagine government as a tree with three big branches.

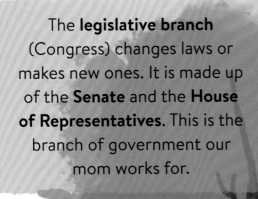

The **legislative branch** (Congress) changes laws or makes new ones. It is made up of the **Senate** and the **House of Representatives**. This is the branch of government our mom works for.

The **judicial branch** is made up of justices (judges) and others who interpret the law and decide what kind of consequences will be given when laws aren't followed.

The **executive branch** is made up of leaders—such as a state governor or the country's president and cabinet. These leaders approve (or veto) and carry out the new laws voted on by Congress, and communicate with other nations.

The House is where Mama has served—both at the state level in Michigan and at the federal level in Washington, D.C.!

To the community that raised me. To my Palestinian family
that gave me wings. To my sons who inspire me.
—R.T.

Thank you, Mama, for saying yes to writing a book together;
Yousif for being a cool little brother; and Baba for teaching me
about my Palestinian roots.
—A.T.

For Rashida, Adam, and Yousif Tlaib, and for all women
and youth finding the courage to speak up
—M.P.

To my parents, for raising me with love and acceptance
—O.A.

Clarion Books is an imprint of HarperCollins Publishers.

Mama in Congress
Text copyright © 2022 by Rashida and Adam Tlaib
Illustrations copyright © 2022 by Olivia Aserr

ISBN 978-0-35-868343-8

Typography by Celeste Knudsen and Jen Keenan
22 23 24 25 26 RTLO 10 9 8 7 6 5 4 3 2 1

First Edition